The Bean Bag Zoo

Collector's Series

7 All-New Elementary Piano Solos for Bean Bag Animal Lovers

CATHERINE ROLLIN

Welcome to The BEAN BAG ZOO Collector's Series! The idea for a BEAN BAG ZOO solo series first came to me when my daughter started collecting bean bag toys. I watched her play with them and saw a magical world of imagination open up. I thought it would be fun to use imagery and tales of Bean Bag animal adventures to help students achieve musical goals. The BEAN BAG ZOO sheet music solos were very well received, resulting in many requests for collections. Thus, this new collector's series features all-new pieces. Just as in the sheet music solos, these two new collections employ visual imagery that helps students succeed with musical concepts. I have found that it is easier to teach a bouncy staccato when a student can picture a leaping frog or a laughing chimp. Spooky sounding crescendos and diminuendos are easy to achieve when a student can envision a mysterious owl in the night. Floating legatos are attainable with the image of a beautiful rainbow fish.

I hope students have as much fun playing in this zoo as I had creating it!

Let's play!

Catherine Rollin

Cover illustration: Beverly Lazor-Bahr

This collection is for the most creative, fun and imaginative person that I know, my daughter, Summer.

My Laughing Chimpanzee

Catherine Rollin

Playfully

Hee - ha - ha - ha! Hee - ho - ho - ho! My laugh-ing chim-pan -

zee, Hee - ha - ha - ha! Hee - ho - ho - ho! He's

smil - ing right at me! Itch - ing, scratch - ing,

jump - ing, laugh - ing, you'd think he had fleas!

13

But this is the way they play all day, the chim-pan - zees! Hee -

17

ha - ha - ha! Hee - ho - ho - ho! My laugh-ing chim-pan - zee, Hee -

21

ha - ha - ha! Hee - ho - ho - ho! He's smil-ing right at me! Hee -

25

ha - ha - ha! Hee - ho - ho - ho! My Bean Bag Chim-pan - zee!

Owl in the Night

Catherine Rollin

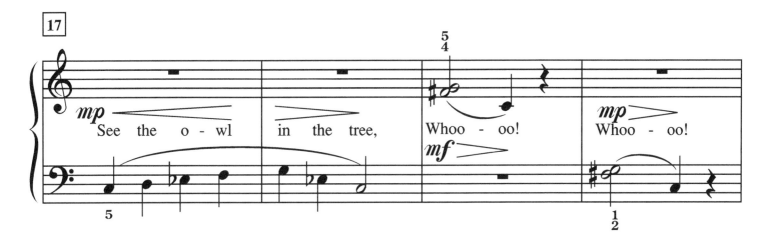

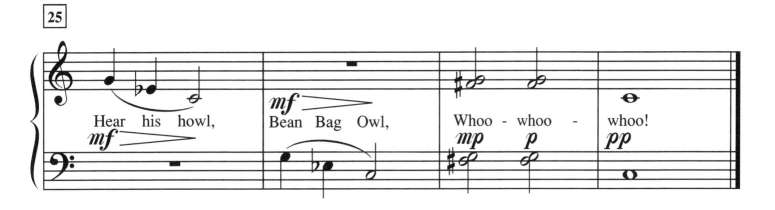

My Frog

Catherine Rollin

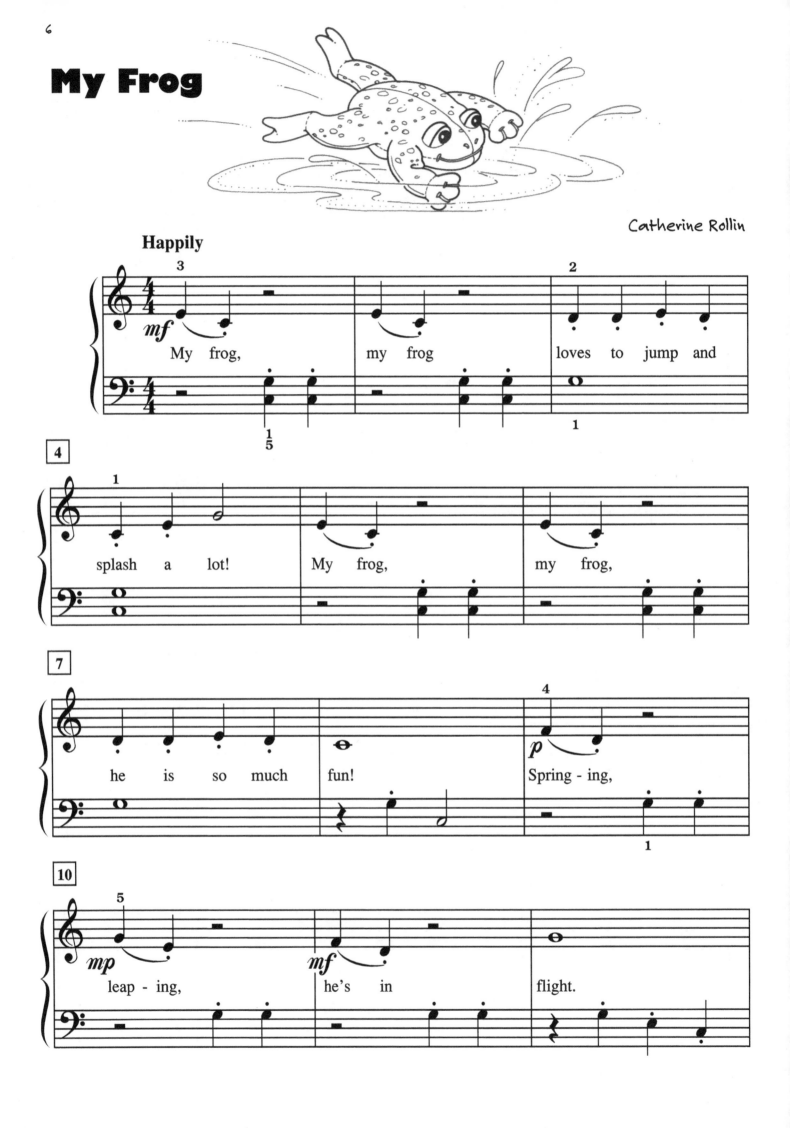

13

p That's my *mp* Bean-Frog, *cresc.* he's got it just *mf* right!

17

My frog, my frog loves to jump and splash a lot!

21

My frog, my frog, he is so much fun!

25

mp My frog, *mf* my frog, *f* Oops! Ker - plop!

8va - - - - - -

Rainbow Fish

Catherine Rollin

Flowing dreamily

hold the damper pedal down throughout

Grace-ful-ly swim-ming through o-ceans of deep, deep, blue, I love

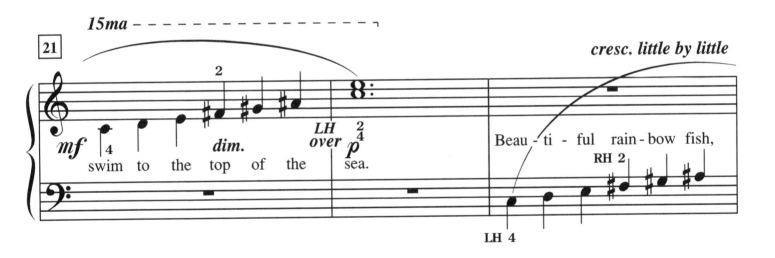

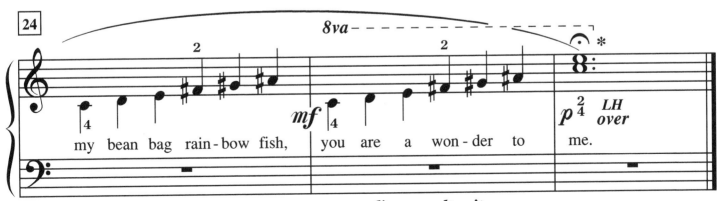

* Hold 𝄐 until sound fades.

Rockin' Raccoon

Catherine Rollin

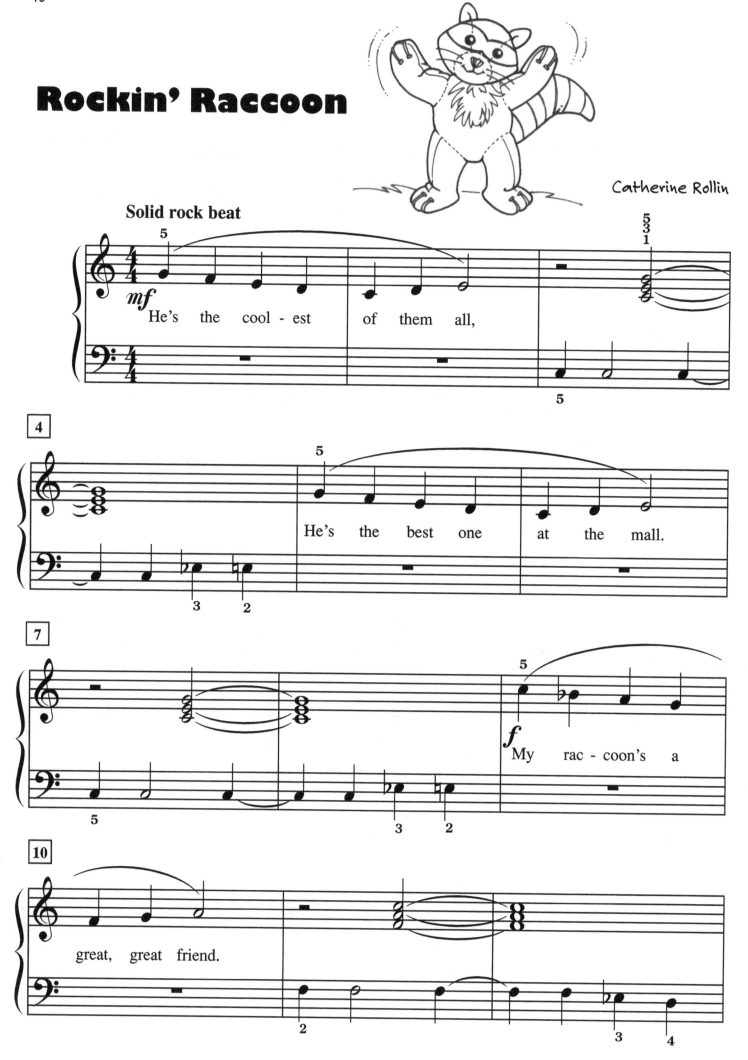

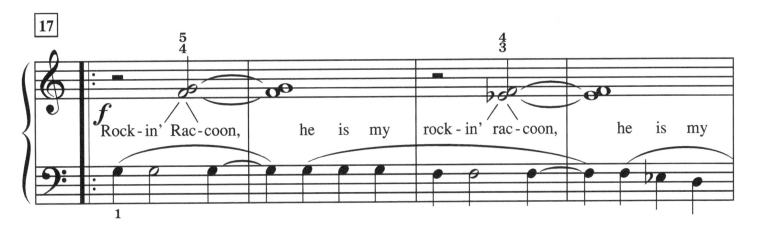

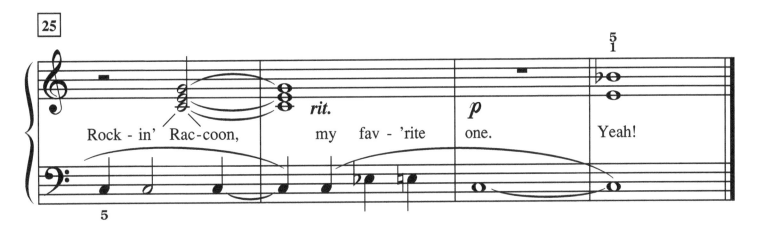

Waltz of the Chicks

Graceful and playful

Catherine Rollin

Both hands one octave higher than written to Coda

See the chicks danc-ing so grace - ful - ly. Waltz - ing now as we play, one, two, three!

to Coda ⊕

Out of their shells, on to their toes,

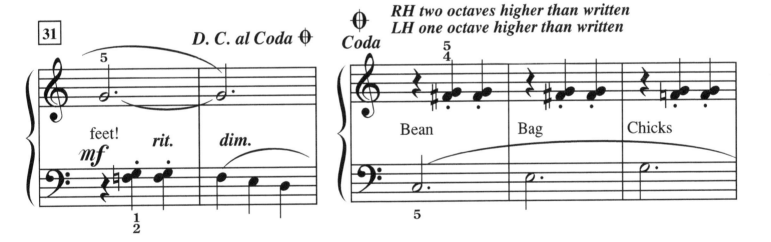

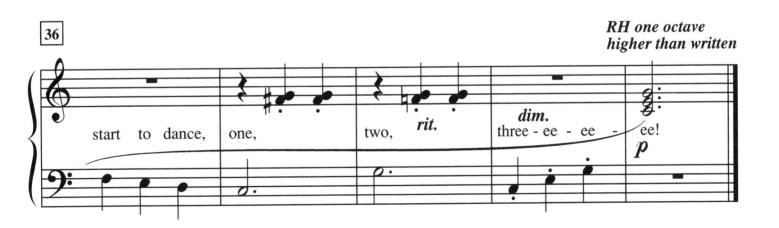

The Millennium Bean Bag Zoo

Catherine Rollin

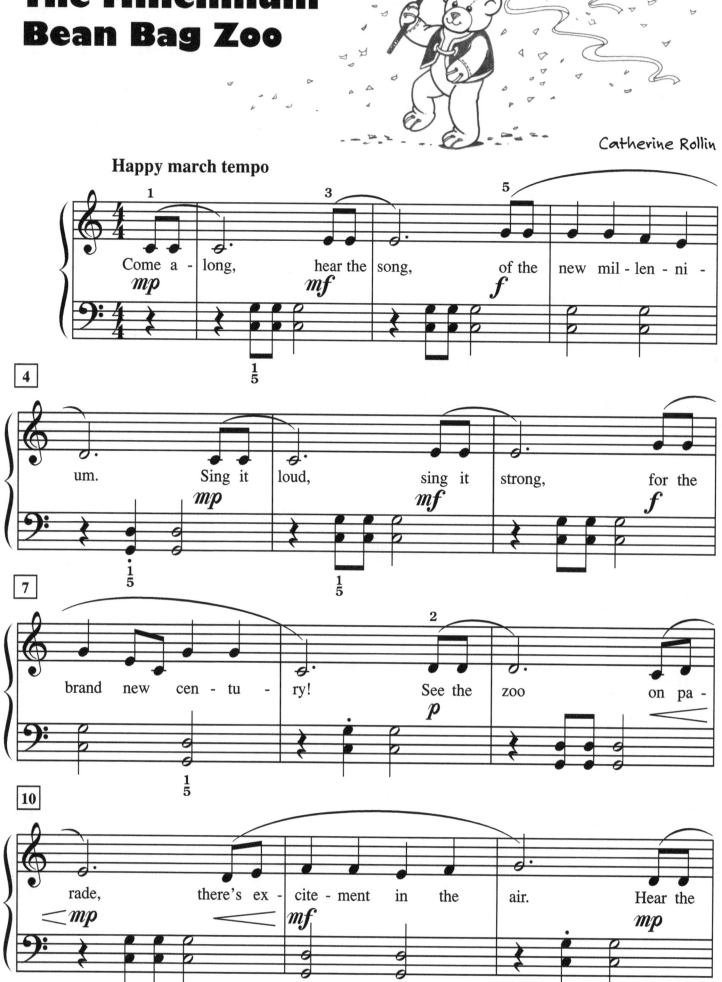

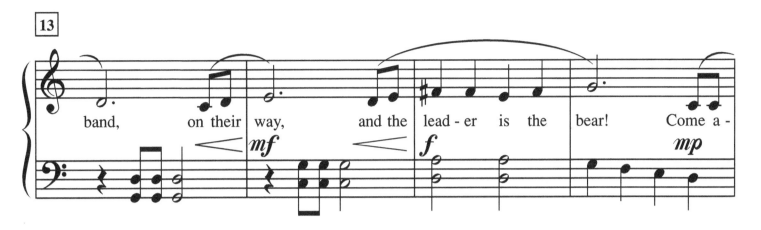

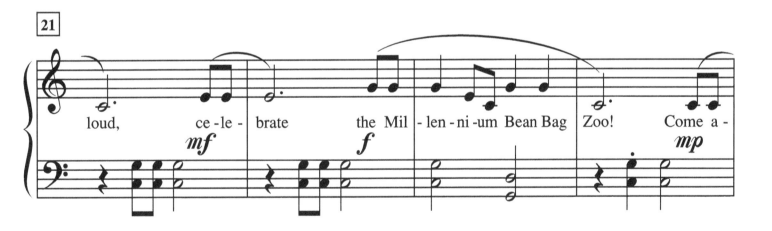

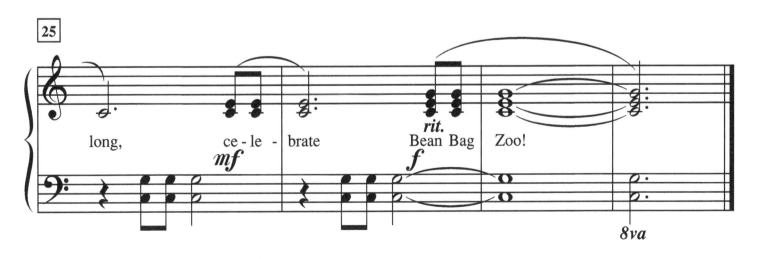